GU00733397

IT Infrastructure Lib

An Introduction to Business Continuity Management

LONDON: HMSO

The Government Centre for
Information Systems

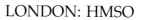

Acknowledgements   The assistance of Simon Marvell under contract to CCTA from Insight Consulting is gratefully acknowledged.

First published 1995
Second impression 1995

ISBN 0 11 330669 5

For further information regarding CCTA products please contact:

CCTA Library
Rosebery Court
St Andrews Business Park
Norwich
NR7 0HS
01 603 704930

Contents

1 About this volume

1.1 Purpose of this volume

Organisations have various ways of judging business success. In the public sector one success criterion is quality of service to the citizen. In the private sector, growth of market share is a success measure. In all sectors, a condition for success is that the business should continue to function in the face of fire, flood and other disasters. The discipline that ensures the business can continue is business continuity management.

This volume describes the need for business continuity management (BCM) and outlines the processes involved. It also describes typical management structures for BCM and explains how to establish a BCM initiative and how to generate awareness and commitment.

The guidance draws on practical experience in BCM from both the public and private sectors. Application of the guidance will help organisations to carry out BCM in accordance with the new British Standard, BS 7799, entitled *A Code of Practice for Information Security Management.*

1.2 Who should read this volume

The volume is intended for managers who are responsible for the performance of business processes and functions. This may include:

- managers of key business processes (such as order processing, sales and customer services) who will have responsibility for the continuity and performance of individual processes

- managers of key support functions such as IT, office services and telecommunications who will have responsibility for the continuity and performance of individual functions

- those people responsible for specifying and managing services from external providers.This guidance may also be of interest to the management services and IS/IT services industry.

| 1.3 | **Structure of the volume** | The remainder of this chapter describes the need for BCM, the benefits it can provide and the importance of senior management commitment. |

Five further chapters set out how the approach can help organisations survive a major disruption to the business:

- Chapter 2 explains the scope of BCM and how it interrelates with business and technical strategic planning and other management disciplines

- Chapter 3 describes the processes involved in BCM and introduces the BCM lifecycle

- Chapter 4 outlines a management structure for BCM

- Chapter 5 explains how to get started with BCM

- Chapter 6 describes how to generate and maintain management support and commitment.

This *Introduction to Business Continuity Management* is complemented by a complete handbook describing how to implement BCM, *A Guide to Business Continuity Management*. Both are volumes from the CCTA IT Infrastructure Library.

BCM issues are highlighted in a CCTA briefing pamphlet for senior management: *Safeguarding the Business – The Role of Business Continuity Management*.

| 1.4 | **The need for BCM** | The modern business environment is characterised by risk. Organisations define objectives, develop strategies and set targets and budgets, yet even the best laid plans can be shattered by unforeseen events. Unfortunately, the chances of an organisation suffering a major disruption to its business are real – incidences of terrorism, disasters, fraud and commercial espionage have all increased in recent years. |

Against this background, most organisations continue to undergo significant change in the hope of becoming more effective and competitive. This often involves reducing overheads (usually staff) and shortening the time taken to handle business transactions or complete business activities. Means of achieving this include:

- re-engineering business processes

- increased automation of business processes

- outsourcing of business functions.

As organisations change, risks change. Whilst certain risks may reduce (increased automation may, for example, reduce the risks from industrial action), re-engineering of business processes can introduce significant new risks, particularly where there is a heavy dependence on technology and external service providers.

Where a disruption affects critical business processes the consequences can be severe and include substantial financial loss, embarrassment and loss of credibility or goodwill for the organisation concerned. The consequential damage can extend much wider; impacting on staff welfare, customers, suppliers, tax payers, shareholders and the general public.

BCM is concerned with managing risks to ensure that at all times an organisation can continue operating to, at least, a pre-determined minimum level.

This management process, BCM, involves reducing the risk to an acceptable level and planning for the recovery of business processes should a risk materialise and a disruption to the business occur.

In some industries, such as financial services, there are growing pressures for regulatory intervention to force the adoption of BCM. Within government, central policies have been formed on the need for continuity planning, at least in regard to IT systems, and the Public Accounts Committee is showing ever greater interest. In other cases, market forces have demanded that key suppliers implement BCM programmes to remain competitive.

Whatever the external forces, BCM must be considered an essential activity for a professional and responsible organisation. Policy on BCM needs to be set at the highest business planning level and integrated with other business and technical policies.

The techniques and the technology for cost effective BCM are available today and the taking of unnecessary risks, whether it be with public money, shareholders' funds, jobs or public health and safety, must be avoided.

1.5 The benefits of BCM	BCM is concerned with the management of risk. Like insurance, BCM is a cost that may not show any tangible reward from year to year but which exists to protect the organisation from the potentially disastrous consequences of a serious disruption to business. With BCM an organisation has planned to survive a major incident that might otherwise have terminated the organisation's ability to function.

The annual spend on BCM is equivalent to an insurance premium and, like insurance, the optimum spend will be determined by the circumstances and risks facing the organisation.

The question is not:

Do we need business continuity management? or

Can we take the risk of not having business continuity management? but

To what extent do we need business continuity management?

BCM allows the organisation to take responsibility for managing its own risks (part of which may be a decision to transfer some of the risk to a third party). This enables an organisation to understand better the environment in which it operates and to act positively to protect the interests of all stakeholders.

A better understanding of risk can pay dividends in other areas, particularly where investment decisions or strategic moves are influenced by risk. An organisation that understands how to assess and manage risk is better placed to take calculated risks. In the public sector, although government organisations do not insure, BCM is a key part of good government and underpins the Citizen's Charter by supporting the consistent and timely delivery of services.

By demonstrating that it has been proactive in reducing risk an organisation may be able to negotiate lower premiums with its insurers. Alternatively if, through BCM, an organisation can limit its potential loss then it can reduce its level of cover or even (as is generally the case in the public sector) decide to bear the loss (self-insure) should a disruption actually occur.

In the early nineties, insurance premiums for terrorist cover rose dramatically but some businesses had enough confidence in their BCM programmes to reduce costs and self-insure at a time when the risk had never been higher.

1.6 Management commitment

BCM is concerned with the performance, and ultimately the survival, of an organisation and is, therefore, a top management issue requiring significant and positive commitment from that level.

All senior managers have a responsibility for ensuring that critical business processes under their control are adequately protected.

Chapter 6 provides guidance on how to secure management commitment and support.

2 The scope of business continuity management

BCM is focused, in the first instance, on entire business processes rather than on particular assets such as IT systems. This is because in order to operate, an organisation must continue to execute its critical business processes. These processes may be contained within one business function, or may integrate or impact on a number of them. Recovery of IT systems alone will not keep such business processes running if staff have no accommodation, if critical paper records have been destroyed or if the organisation cannot communicate with its customers and suppliers.

Achievement of an agreed optimum level of operation following a major business disruption will require critical business processes to continue to run to that level. This, in turn, will require a commensurate provision of staff, accommodation, IT systems, paper records, communications, power and other critical equipment and services for each critical business process.

Figure 1 illustrates how the degree of dependence can vary for different business processes. Process A is heavily dependent on information and systems, whilst Process B has a greater reliance on staff, accommodation and suppliers.

Organisations can be heavily dependent on external service providers. The effect of a disruption at one service provider can ripple all the way up the supply chain through the organisation to its customers and back to other service providers.

It is possible that following a disruption, business processes will need to change for a period to enable a minimum service to be provided, for example a predominantly automated process (eg order processing) may revert to a manual method of working until an automated process can be resumed.

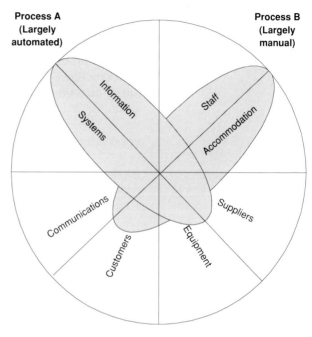

Figure 1: The scope of BCM

There are three key elements to BCM:

- reduction or avoidance of identified risks (on the basis that prevention is better than cure)

- planning for the recovery of business processes should a risk materialise and a business disruption occur

- transference of all or part of the risk to an insurer or other third party (for example, via outsourcing or, in government, the private finance initiative).

Insurance is an important element of planning for business continuity but should only be considered as providing compensation when other means of managing the risk have been exhausted. Within government, insurance requires careful cost justification and approval from HM Treasury.

2.1   Relationship with business and technical strategies

Business and technical strategies will provide much information to a BCM initiative. They are likely to highlight objectives and success factors, and identify key business processes, functions and technical infrastructures. Most importantly, they will identify future directions that will need to be accommodated within the business continuity strategy.

Although comparatively rare, there may be circumstances when BCM considerations might heavily influence the adopted strategic direction. Conversely, changes in the business or technical strategies are likely to have significant implications for the business continuity strategy. BCM should, therefore, be closely coupled with the strategic planning processes in order that it can be reassessed as the strategy changes.

2.2   Relationship with contingency planning and disaster recovery

The terms contingency planning and disaster recovery planning are often interchanged with business continuity management. Both of these terms are limited in that they imply recovery planning (to the exclusion of risk reduction and wider issues of availability management) and the latter implies a physical disaster. The terms also tend to be used in relation to IT assets rather than complete business processes. The activities in contingency planning and disaster recovery planning are encompassed within BCM but the scope of BCM is wider, taking a holistic and comprehensive view of the business.

2.3   Relationship with security management

Some elements of BCM are very closely related to security management. For example:

- risk reduction measures (such as access controls) will be required in security management to protect the confidentiality and integrity of information and the safety of staff, and in BCM to protect the availability of critical business processes

- similar business impact and risk analysis techniques are used to determine requirements for security and for business continuity

- similar skills are required to manage the operational processes in security and business continuity management – in many organisations these are undertaken by the same function

• security is an important part of business recovery planning – the opportunities for fraud and theft may increase during times of crisis.

Improved efficiency and effectiveness may therefore be achieved by providing a level of integration between the BCM, security and insurance functions.

| 2.4 | **Determining the scope of BCM** | The scope of BCM activities within an organisation will be determined by factors that are specific to its particular circumstances. These factors will include: |

The scope of BCM activities within an organisation will be determined by factors that are specific to its particular circumstances. These factors will include:

• the dependence of the organisation on technology, human resources or external suppliers

• the number of critical business processes and the degree of integration between them

• the organisation's operational and geographic structure

• the organisation's attitude to risk.

At the broadest level, the scope of BCM is usually defined in terms of the:

• business processes to be covered and their key components, such as information, systems, staff

• risks to be addressed.

The initial focus is likely to be placed on management's view of the more critical business processes and the greatest risks. Once these have been identified and investigated, the scope may be narrowed to concentrate on the most vulnerable points of failure within the critical processes.

2.4.1 Risks within the scope of BCM

The risks covered by BCM tend to be those that could result in a sudden and serious disruption to the business, for example:

- damage or denial of access to premises, perhaps as a result of terrorism, fire or other physical disasters

- loss of critical services such as telecommunications and power

- failure or non-performance of critical suppliers, distributors or other third parties, particularly where key business functions have been outsourced

- human error, technical or environmental breakdown

- fraud, sabotage, extortion or commercial espionage

- deliberate infiltration of IT systems by viruses or other forms of malicious software

- industrial action or other unavailability of key staff.

2.4.2 Risks outside the scope of BCM

BCM does not usually encompass longer term risks such as those from competitors and regulators, risks relating to expansion, diversification, restructuring and so on. Whilst the implications of these risks can be serious, management usually has some time to identify and evaluate the risk and take some action to prevent a risk becoming a problem.

BCM also does not usually cover risks at the other end of the spectrum such as minor technical faults, except where there is a possibility that the impact could escalate to such a level that it threatened the business. The most common reasons for invoking IT recovery services relate to upgrades or other changes that have gone wrong. The disciplines of availability management, problem management and change management are usually applied to these types of risk. However BCM will provide the ultimate safety-net should a problem turn into a disaster.

It is clear that a successful organisation will need to manage the complete spectrum of risks that it may face.

3   What is business continuity management?

The BCM lifecycle consists of four distinct stages:

- **Stage 1 – Initiation**, which sets policy for BCM, ensures that it is integrated with other business and technical policies and establishes the BCM initiative

- **Stage 2 – Requirements and Strategy**, which assesses the potential business impacts and risks, identifies and evaluates options for reducing risk and recovering business processes and develops a cost effective strategy for BCM

- **Stage 3 – Implementation**, which establishes a programme by which business continuity will be achieved, implements the stand-by facilities and risk reduction measures specified within the BCM strategy, develops the requisite business recovery plans and procedures and undertakes initial testing

- **Stage 4 – Operational Management**, which ensures that the business continuity strategy, plans and procedures continue to be tested, reviewed and maintained on an on-going basis and that suitable training and awareness programmes are put in place.

Each stage consists of one or more processes. A process model for BCM is shown in Figure 2. The Maturity Levels shown in Figure 2 are described in section 3.4.

Chapter 5 covers Stage 1 of the lifecycle in some detail. The processes within the remaining stages of the BCM lifecycle are outlined in Figure 2.

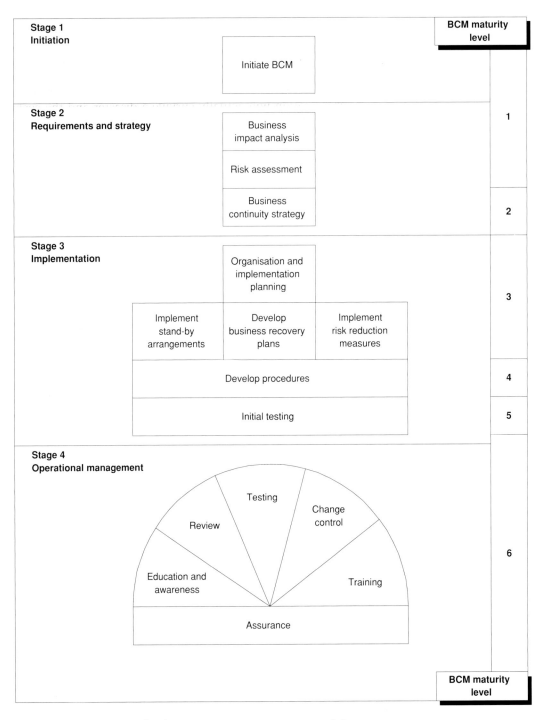

Figure 2: Business continuity management process model

3.1 Stage 2 – Requirements analysis and strategy definition

At this stage in BCM, business requirements and risks are assessed and decisions are taken on the optimum approach to manage business continuity within the organisation. It is a critical stage in the BCM lifecycle since decisions taken here will determine how well the organisation will actually survive a disaster and the costs that the organisation will incur on BCM. Any errors or omissions at this stage will have serious implications at a later stage in the lifecycle.

The requirements analysis and strategy definition stage consists of the following processes:

- perform business impact analysis

- perform risk assessment

- develop business continuity strategy.

The activities within each process are described in the following sections.

Business impact analysis

A key driver in determining BCM requirements is *how much the organisation stands to lose* as a result of a disaster or other incident and how quickly these losses would materialise. This can be assessed through a business impact analysis.

The purpose of a business impact analysis is to identify:

- critical business processes

- the potential damage or loss that may be caused to the organisation as a result of a disruption to critical business processes.

The business impact analysis will also identify:

- the form that the damage or loss may take, eg lost income, additional costs, loss of goodwill

- how the degree of damage or loss is likely to escalate with time in the aftermath of an incident

- the minimum staffing, facilities and services necessary to enable business processes to continue operating at a minimum acceptable level

- the time within which minimum levels of staffing, facilities and services should be recovered

- the time within which business processes and all supporting staff, facilities and services should be fully recovered.

Impacts are measured against particular scenarios for each business process. Example scenarios are:

- customer services cannot operate for X hours

- invoicing is delayed by Y days.

The impact analysis will concentrate on the scenarios where the impact on critical business processes is likely to be greatest.

Business impacts will be measured against the scenarios and will typically fall into one or more of the following categories:

- failure to achieve agreed service levels

- financial loss

- additional costs

- long term loss of market share

- breach of the law

- risk to personal safety

- political, corporate or personal embarrassment

- loss of goodwill

- loss of credibility

- loss of operational capability, for example in a command and control environment.

The impact valuations will allow conclusions to be drawn on the maximum time for which disruption could be tolerated by the organisation. Taking the examples given above an organisation may decide that:

- it could not withstand unavailability of customer services for more than two hours

- invoicing must not be delayed by more than two weeks.

In many cases, business processes can be re-established without the full complement of staff, systems and other assets – often an equivalent to the 80/20 per cent rule will apply. Business recovery objectives should therefore be stated in terms of:

- the time within which a pre-defined team of core staff and stated minimum facilities must be recovered

- the timetable for recovery of remaining staff and facilities.

The business recovery objectives (as stated at this stage) cannot always be met. It may for example prove too expensive to provide the necessary stand-by arrangements. The recovery objectives will, however, form the starting point from which different recovery options can be evaluated.

Risk assessment

The second key driver in determining BCM requirements is *the likelihood that a disaster or other serious incident will actually occur*. This is a function of the level of threat and the extent of the organisation's vulnerability to each threat.

Threats and vulnerabilities relate to particular components of the business process. For example an organisation might decide that the impact scenario, customer services cannot operate for X hours, could result from:

- disaster or denial of access to location A (eg where critical computer systems are located) which might be owned by an external service provider

- disaster or denial of access to location B (eg where the customer services function is located)

- loss of power or telecommunications services to either site

- failure of a critical computer system

- industrial action by customer services staff, and so on.

The level of threat will depend on factors such as:

- likely motivation, capability and resources for deliberate incidents, such as bombings, arson, espionage, industrial action

- for accidental incidents, the organisation's location, environment, and quality of internal systems and procedures.

Business processes are highly vulnerable where there are critical single points of failure, typical examples of which are:

- a concentration of high proportions of staff, systems, records and other critical assets in a single geographic location

- a reliance upon individual service providers

- dependence upon individuals or small groups of people for critical business activities

- communications networks with no inbuilt resilience.

Guidance on how to measure business impacts and risks can be found in the CCTA Management of Risk Library and in the CCTA Risk Analysis and Management Method (CRAMM).

Business continuity
strategy

The impact analysis and risk assessment will provide the
information from which the business continuity strategy
will be developed. Without these complementary items
of information, it is unlikely that the optimum balance of
risk reduction and recovery planning will be obtained or
an appropriate strategy selected.

Following the impact analysis and risk assessment it will
be possible to identify a number of options through
which the BCM requirements of the organisation could
be met. Typical business recovery options (which could
be invoked in tandem) are as follows:

- recovery options for accommodation
  - other premises owned or leased by the
    organisation
  - premises belonging to suppliers or other third
    parties/partners
  - commercial business recovery services
  - staff to work from home
  - reciprocal arrangements with other organisations
  - rapid identification and procurement of
    alternative accommodation after any disaster

- recovery options for IT systems and networks
  - procure stand-by equipment and house off-site in
    a secure location
  - call-off contracts to guarantee delivery of new
    equipment within agreed timescale post disaster
  - reciprocal agreements within the organisation or
    with third parties
  - commercial systems recovery services involving
    fall-back onto fixed systems operated by the
    systems recovery supplier or the provision of a
    stand-by mobile service
  - rush orders for replacement equipment to be
    placed post disaster.

The CCTA IT Infrastructure Library guide on
Contingency Planning provides further details on options
for IT systems.

- Recovery options for external service providers
  - require service providers to implement BCM to a level that is acceptable to the customer
  - plan to fall back to alternative suppliers in the event of a major disruption affecting the primary supplier.

Options will also need to be considered for people; for other critical assets such as paper records, reference material and other equipment; for critical services such as power, telecommunications, post; and for critical service suppliers.

Options for systems and some other assets will be reliant on an effective back-up policy to ensure that critical software, data and documentation are not lost.

A cost/benefit/risk analysis should be undertaken for each option. This will involve a comparative assessment of the:

- ability to meet business recovery objectives

- likely reduction in the potential impact

- cost of setting up the option

- cost of maintaining, testing and invoking the option

- technical, organisational, cultural and administrative implications against the risk of disruption or disaster and the potential impact if no action is taken.

Care should also be taken to ensure that the introduction of an option to address one particular risk does not increase the risks in other areas.

Where insurance against particular risks is in place, or is available to the organisation (some organisations self-insure), this will need to be taken into account during analysis of options. However, care should be taken to avoid overstating the value of insurance – loss adjustors will attempt to reduce the claim and payment may take some time. Insurance is unlikely to compensate fully for long term or intangible business impacts. Options for risk reduction measures will also be identified and evaluated during this process.

Typical risk reduction options will include:

- improvements in resilience of business functions and processes by eliminating single points of failure

- limiting the amount of business given to any one provider of external services

- building fault tolerance and resilience into IT systems and networks

- implementing additional security such as access control or CCTV to deter or detect deliberate physical attacks

- providing additional controls to detect local incidents such as fire, flood etc before serious damage occurs

- improving procedures to reduce the likelihood of errors or failures, eg project management, structured systems design, configuration management, change control, incident reporting, escalation procedures.

The security management function may also be considering similar measures, for particular IT systems, and hence additional justification for these measures may be possible.

The business continuity strategy will be determined by selecting a suitable balance of risk reduction and business recovery options to minimise the risks and meet the business recovery objectives. It is important that organisations check that recovery options selected are capable of implementation and integration at the time they are required, and that the services required to recover hang together and are capable of being introduced under the control of the organisation.

It may be found, during analysis of options, that the business recovery objectives, as specified during the impact analysis, cannot be achieved in a cost effective manner. Trade-offs may be necessary between the potential impacts that could result from a disaster and the cost of providing for business recovery. Some relaxation in the business recovery objectives may therefore be necessary to enable a cost-effective strategy to be formulated.

If expenditure can be delayed until a disruption occurs, whilst still achieving business recovery within an acceptable time, this is likely to be the most attractive option because:

- the disruption may never occur

- where insurance is in place, additional costs incurred after the disruption occurs may be recoverable

- any costs incurred in advance will not be recoverable.

Risk assessment methods (such as CRAMM) which also address risk management will assist with the identification and analysis of both risk reduction and business recovery options.

3.2 Stage 3 – Implementation

Having defined and gained agreement to the business continuity strategy, the BCM lifecycle moves into the implementation stage. This involves implementation of stand-by and risk reduction arrangements and the development of the required recovery plans and procedures to support them.

The implementation stage consists of the following processes:

- establish organisation and develop implementation plans (section 3.2.1)

- implement stand-by arrangements (section 3.2.2)

- implement risk reduction measures (section 3.2.3)

- develop business recovery plans (section 3.2.4)

- develop procedures (section 3.2.5)

- carry out initial tests (section 3.2.6).

3.2.1 Establish organisation and develop implementation plans

The activities in this process are:

- establish command, control and communications structure

- develop framework for business recovery plans

- develop implementation plans.

Establish command, control and communications structure

A clear structure for command, control and communications will need to be established to control business recovery activities following a major business disruption. Recent case studies have highlighted problems that can occur when lines of communication break down or become confused. Lines of communication between various business recovery teams and the top executive or management Board and the means by which they will be established must be specified and agreed. Figure 3 illustrates how a command, control and communications structure might be established with:

- the top management/executive Board retaining overall authority and control within the organisation and responsible for crisis management and liaison with other departments/group organisations or companies, the media, regulators, influential contacts, etc

- a separate central co-ordination team, typically comprising people at one level below the top management/executive Board, responsible for co-ordinating the overall recovery effort within the organisation

- a series of business recovery teams, typically representing each critical business function, responsible for executing business recovery plans for their own areas and for day to day liaison with staff, customers and suppliers.

The roles and responsibilities at each level of the command, control and communications structure will need to be defined carefully.

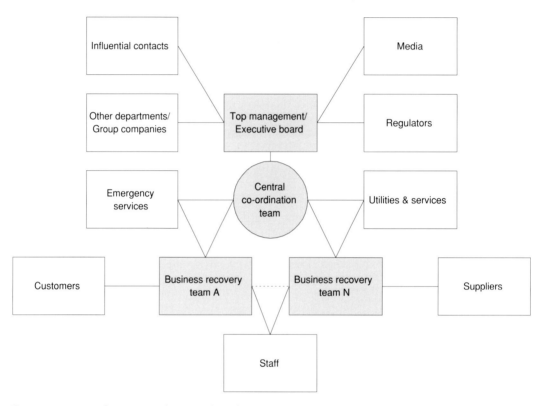

Figure 3: Typical command control and communications structure

Define framework for business recovery plans

A business recovery plan (or more often an integrated set of plans) will describe the actions to be taken from the moment that a disruption occurs. The plan(s) will typically cover activities such as emergency response, crisis management, damage assessment, salvage, deciding on whether or not to invoke stand-by arrangements, invocation of stand-by arrangements, recovery of business processes and, eventually, return-to-normal.

The business recovery plans will, typically, contain a description of roles and responsibilities, action lists and reference data, often structured into discrete phases.

To enable an integrated set of plans to be produced and to achieve a common standard it is usually beneficial to develop and agree a business recovery plan framework before moving on to produce the detailed plans. The framework will describe the complete set of plans to be produced and how they will be structured. Ideally, the framework will include plan templates which can be taken and completed by the relevant individual or team.

Construction of the framework will take account of the agreed command, control and communications structure and also future maintenance requirements.

Figure 4 illustrates the recovery activities that typically need to be carried out, starting with emergency response and running through to eventual return-to-normal. These activities are shown grouped into three broad phases: Alert; Invocation and recovery; and Return-to-normal. Crisis management is undertaken across all three phases. Figure 4 also describes typical plan content and shows how business recovery plans may be structured.

Develop
implementation plans

Implementation plans will be necessary to co-ordinate implementation of stand-by and risk reduction measures, and the development and management of business recovery plans, across several business functions.

3.2.2 Implement stand-by
arrangements

Certain actions are likely to be necessary to implement the selected stand-by arrangements, for example:

- preparing and equipping stand-by accommodation

- purchasing and installing stand-by computer systems

- negotiating with external service providers on their BCM arrangements, and auditing them if possible

- selecting suppliers of commercial recovery services and negotiating contracts.

Training and new procedures may be required to operate, test and maintain the stand-by arrangements and to ensure that they are ready to be called into action when required.

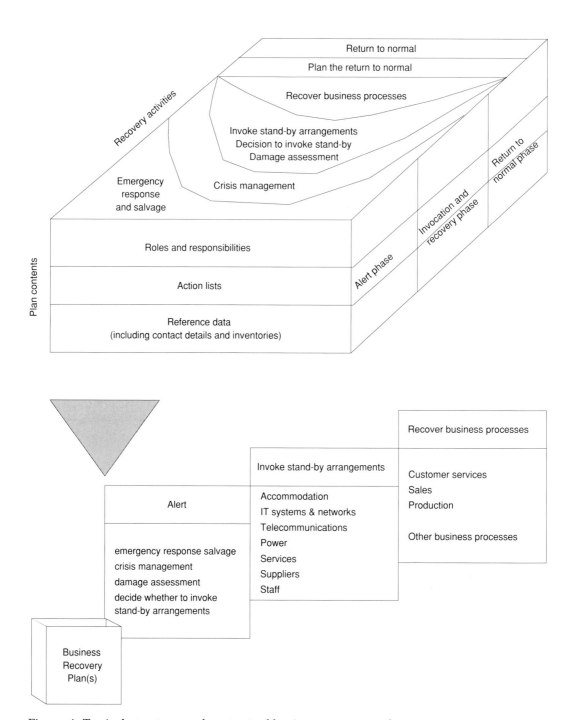

Figure 4: Typical structure and content of business recovery plans

| 3.2.3 | Implement risk reduction measures | Any additional risk reduction measures defined in the strategy will need to be implemented. The activities involved in this are common to any procurement and/or implementation exercise. Other CCTA guidance (such as the Management of Risk library, PRINCE and, for application software, SSADM) covers these activities in some detail. |

Some risk reduction measures will themselves be procedures. As with stand-by arrangements, training and new procedures may also be required to operate, test and maintain physical risk reduction measures.

| 3.2.4 | Develop business recovery plan(s) | Business recovery plans will be produced by completing the plan templates included as part of the business recovery plan framework (see Figure 4). This completion activity will involve: |

- including the actions which will need to be carried out by each team or team member

- including, or cross-referring to, any reference data which may be needed to complete the actions, eg: contact details for staff, suppliers, customers; inventory details for accommodation, equipment, communications, systems, data; other relevant information.

The action lists should not be over-complicated or too detailed but should clearly specify the actions that are required. It is possible that staff may have been killed or injured, in which case roles will need to be filled by deputies. Reference data should be only that which will be essential to support the recovery effort – reference data that could be obtained from other sources or re-created easily can be omitted from the plans.

| 3.2.5 | Develop procedures | Action lists must be distinguished from the detailed business recovery procedures which may be necessary to support particular actions and also from the detailed procedures that a business function might follow to run its business in an emergency. Procedures tend to relate to complex activities that must be undertaken differently, or which are only required, in an emergency situation. Examples include: |

- manual procedures for the recording of orders, credit checking and issuing of invoices

- procedures for damage assessment, salvage and restoration

- procedures for the emergency transfer of business from one external service provider to another

- procedures to install and test replacement hardware and networks and to restore software and data to a common reference point which is consistent across all business processes.

Such procedures will be fundamental to ensuring effective recovery of the business in line with recovery objectives.

3.2.6   Initial testing

Testing is a critical part of the overall BCM process and is the only way of ensuring that the selected strategy, stand-by arrangements, business recovery plans and procedures will work in practice.

Business recovery tests can typically be categorised into four types:

- walkthroughs, a paper exercise in which a team, or teams, work to a set scenario

- technical component tests, in which specific technical components of the strategy and plans are tested. Technical component tests can often be undertaken without significant involvement from users in business functions

- business component tests, in which the recovery of an individual business process or business function is tested. This must always involve the business functions concerned

- full tests, which will replicate, as closely as possible, the invocation of all stand-by arrangements and the recovery of business processes.

All tests will be undertaken against defined test scenarios which will be described as realistically as possible. It should be noted, however, that even the most comprehensive test will not cover everything. For example, it is not possible to test realistically the way in which staff will react in a crisis when colleagues may have been injured or killed and the business recovery plans will need to make an allowance for this.

**3.3   Stage 4 –
         Operational
         management**

On completion of the implementation and planning stage, the BCM lifecycle moves into operational management of business continuity. This is a set of ongoing BCM processes rather than the project related work that characterised stages 2 and 3.

The operational management stage consists of the following processes:

- education and awareness

- training

- review

- testing

- change control

- assurance.

Education and
awareness

Education and awareness within the organisation of business continuity policy, strategies and plans will be essential for the ongoing success of the BCM initiative. The aim must be to get to a situation where management consider the business continuity implications of all major business activities as part of their normal routine. This process is covered separately in Chapter 6.

Training

In addition to education and awareness, certain staff may require specific training, for example:

- on alternative processes or technology that may be used in an emergency

- on a manual system that may be used whilst an automated system is being recovered

- technical training for certain deputy team members to ensure that they have the required level of competence to facilitate recovery.

Review

All deliverables from the BCM lifecycle will need to be reviewed regularly to ensure that they remain up to date. Different types of review will be required from time to time:

- whenever there is a significant change to the business which could affect the BCM deliverables, eg major change in strategy, reorganisation

- whenever there is a major change to the organisation's assets or dependencies, eg new systems or networks, changed service providers

- whenever the extent of risk facing the organisation is perceived to have changed

- in any case, on a regular basis.

Many organisations have a high rate of change and therefore need to make a significant investment in an ongoing review programme.

Testing

Following on from initial testing, an ongoing programme of testing will be required with the objective that critical components of the business continuity strategy should be tested at least once a year.

Tests can become progressively more demanding over time, for example:

- starting with tests where staff are warned in advance and moving on to those which are initiated without warning

- starting with tests where all primary staff participate and moving on to those where primary staff are prohibited from taking part.

Careful planning will be required for all tests to ensure that they do not, themselves, result in a major disruption to the business.

Change control

BCM deliverables will need to be updated following tests and reviews and in response to day to day changes affecting action lists, reference data and procedures associated with the business recovery plans.

Change control procedures will be necessary to ensure that changes are detected and reflected in the BCM deliverables. This will be achieved by employing a comprehensive change management system to control all changes within the organisation.

Further guidance is provided in the CCTA IT Infrastructure Library guide on *Change Management*.

Assurance

The final process in the BCM lifecycle involves obtaining assurance that the quality of the BCM deliverables is acceptable to senior business management and that the operational management processes are working satisfactorily.

3.4 Key milestones in BCM

Within the BCM lifecycle, six key milestones, or levels of maturity, have been identified whereby organisations can monitor their progress.

1 Completion of an impact analysis and risk assessment.

2 Definition and agreement of a business continuity strategy.

3 Implementation of stand-by arrangements and risk reduction measures, and the development of business recovery plans.

4 Development and implementation of supporting procedures.

5 A successful initial test of the risk reduction measures, stand-by arrangements and business recovery plans.

6 Establishment of successful management processes to test, review, maintain and audit all BCM deliverables.

Movement from one milestone to the next is a significant step in an organisation's progress with BCM and represents a higher level of confidence in the BCM process.

By the time an organisation reaches level six, it will have a high level of confidence that it can respond effectively to a sudden and serious incident.

Movements between one level and the next tend to be the points at which BCM initiatives falter, as difficulties arise, either in 'moving on' or in maintaining commitment and interest. Only at level six does BCM become an intrinsic and relatively subconscious corporate activity. When this level is reached, it is unlikely that any incident will cause catastrophe or place the organisation at significant risk. The management challenge is then to remain at this level and avoid falling back to an earlier level. Provided that the lifecycle approach is maintained, this problem can be avoided.

4   The management structure for business continuity management

Since BCM is concerned with the performance, and ultimately the survival, of an organisation it is a top management issue. By its nature, BCM crosses organisational boundaries and will consume management time and financial resources but these should be in proportion to the risks facing the organisation. Sponsorship at the highest level and an effective management structure are, therefore, critical to the success of any BCM initiative. Without an active sponsor at the top of the organisation there will be a risk that:

- the business continuity strategy will not reflect the true values and risks as perceived by senior management

- the BCM initiative will not be given sufficient momentum, profile or resources to develop into a successful management discipline

- the extensive co-operation and input required from senior and junior management will not be forthcoming.

As a result of this, investment in BCM could be wasted and, more importantly, the organisation might not be able to survive a major disruption to its business.

BCM will only be successful within an organisation if a suitable management structure is in place. The optimum management structure will:

- enable responsibilities for ongoing BCM to be clearly defined and allocated

- give ownership of business continuity strategies and plans to those who are most dependent on them, ie, to business functions

- integrate easily with other existing management structures and hierarchies

- avoid concentrating responsibility in isolated centres of excellence

- allocate responsibility to functions or individuals that have the necessary presence and credibility within the organisation

- ensure that the management structure that manages business continuity on an ongoing basis closely resembles the structure that will control and facilitate business recovery should the business recovery plans have to be put into action.

One of the biggest mistakes that can be made in BCM is to build, develop and maintain plans in isolation from the business functions which they will support. These plans typically fail when they are invoked.

Conversely, considerable benefits in terms of awareness, education, and plan effectiveness can be achieved by spreading responsibility throughout the organisation.

4.1   Responsibilities

Responsibility for BCM touches all parts of the organisation. Figure 5 describes typical responsibilities for BCM during times of normal operation.

Following a disruption to the business, management responsibilities will change in line with the command, control and communications structure and the roles and responsibilities outlined in the business recovery plans. Typical responsibilities during times of crisis are shown in Figure 6.

A management structure is required which will allow these responsibilities to be carried out in an effective and efficient manner.

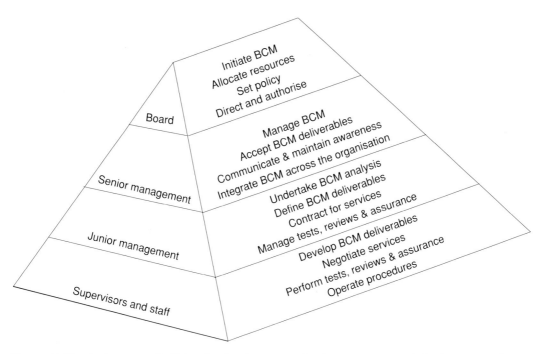

Figure 5: Typical responsibilities for business continuity management during normal operation

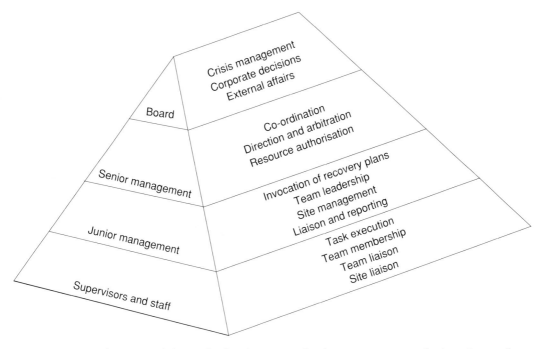

Figure 6: Typical responsibilities for business continuity management during times of crisis

4.2 Management structure

A typical management structure for large organisations that will support both ongoing management of business continuity and invocation of business continuity plans is shown in Figure 7.

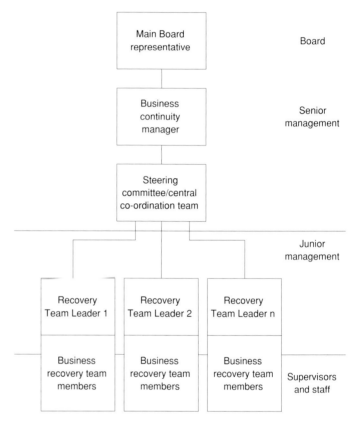

Figure 7: Typical management structure for business continuity

Management responsibility for BCM at Board level will, typically, be given to a person whose responsibilities include those that are already organisation-wide such as finance, IT or facilities.

Day to day responsibility for business continuity may fall to a senior manager (shown in Figure 7 as the business continuity manager) who will:

• advise the Board on BCM strategy and policy

- check that the business continuity strategy and plans remain up to date and effective

- ensure that change control, testing, auditing, awareness and training programmes are established.

In larger organisations, the business continuity manager may be supported by junior management for day to day activities.

Since BCM touches on all parts of a business, many organisations have established steering committees at senior management level to co-ordinate business continuity activities across the organisation. As part of the ongoing management of business continuity, the steering committee would meet regularly to:

- confirm that the business continuity strategy is still valid and that BCM deliverables are being maintained

- ensure that changes which could affect the strategy, eg acquisitions, implementation of a new system, re-location of staff, are addressed

- review and agree a test programme

- initiate any actions necessary to address upcoming changes or to resolve difficulties.

Senior management will typically be given ownership of the BCM deliverables that relate to their business functions, eg the business recovery plan for the Customer Services Function will be owned by the Customer Services Director, the IT Plan by the IT Director and so on. Ownership will involve responsibility for ensuring that the deliverables remain up to date and fit for their purpose.

Steering committee members will also, typically, fill key roles in the central co-ordination team within the command, control and communications structure during times of crisis. The business continuity manager will, typically, chair the Steering Committee and lead the central co-ordination team.

Invocation of stand-by arrangements and recovery of business processes will usually be undertaken by a series of business recovery teams led by junior management. During periods of operational stability the business recovery teams will play a major role in implementing, testing and maintaining stand-by arrangements and risk reduction measures, and in the development, testing and maintenance of business recovery plans.

The approach described above allows the management structure during periods of operational stability to translate easily to the command, control and communications structure required during times of crisis. This, in turn, will facilitate commitment, education and awareness. Indeed, the cross-functional nature of BCM makes it a powerful force towards corporate integration and effective working relationships.

5 Establishing a business continuity management initiative

If BCM is being introduced to the organisation for the first time attention must be focused on securing top management support and commitment – this is the subject of Chapter 6. As soon as practically possible, senior management should set policy for BCM and communicate this throughout the organisation. Suitable organisational and project structures for BCM should then be established and provided with the necessary personnel and financial resources.

Formal initiation of BCM is a key stage in the lifecycle since the way in which BCM is introduced and established in an organisation will influence its likely success.

The introduction of BCM to an organisation will usually be in the form of a project, or programme of projects, to address stages 1, 2 and 3 of the lifecycle. Important considerations in initiating a BCM project are:

- how should the project be organised and controlled?

- what is the scope and terms of reference?

- what methodology will be used?

- what skills are required?

- what resources will be required?

- how should existing contingency plans be incorporated into BCM?

A typical organisational structure for a business continuity project will have a Board level sponsor, a Steering Committee acting as or steering a PRINCE Project Board, a Project Manager, Project Team member(s) and, possibly, a number of working groups to undertake the detailed analysis.

The scope of a BCM project is usually defined with reference to the following:

- which business processes and functions are covered and which locations, buildings, services and assets?

- which risks are covered – just those relating to denial of access to buildings or loss of key assets, or wider, for example, covering disasters at suppliers, industrial action, extortion?

The terms of reference and methodology for the business continuity project will typically mirror the BCM processes described in Chapter 3. Further details can be found in the CCTA *Guide to Business Continuity Management*. The methodology for stage 2 of the lifecycle is supported by CRAMM.

5.1   Skills

BCM embraces many business functions and therefore careful consideration needs to be given to the choice of project manager and selection of the project team.

The following skills and knowledge will be required from project team members:

- good understanding of the business and key business processes or an ability to assimilate this quickly

- good all round understanding of supporting infrastructures, eg provision of accommodation, office services, IT systems, telecommunications

- knowledge of the methodology to be used and the techniques involved in each stage of the BCM lifecycle, eg business impact analysis, risk assessment

- ability to deal with management and staff at all levels.

The steering committee should include representatives from each business process within the scope of the project and from each supporting function, eg IT, office services. Steering committee members are typically drawn from management at one layer below the Board. These people will, collectively, have a sound understanding of the business and its inter-relationships but also have direct management control over the junior management who will provide much of the required information.

5.2   Resources

The resources required for a project to address stages 1, 2 and 3 of the lifecycle will depend on the size and complexity of the business and the scope of the project. Resources will include:

- management and staff time

- capital and revenue spend on stand-by and risk reduction arrangements

- possibly, expenditure on consultancy support, training or specialist software.

As a broad guide, assuming that the project is provided with adequate human and financial resources, completion of stages 1 to 3 of the lifecycle is likely to take a minimum of six months and, possibly, up to two years. Implementation of stand-by arrangements and initial testing are two of the processes that tend to extend the elapsed time required.

BCM is an ongoing management discipline and once the requisite strategy, risk reduction measures, stand-by arrangements, plans and procedures have been developed, and initial testing has been completed, the project will give way to the ongoing management of business continuity (stage 4 of the lifecycle). Some of the processes in stage 4 (such as change control) will be undertaken as day to day management activities. Others (such as annual reviews or tests) may be undertaken as specific projects as part of an overall programme. The resource requirements for stage 4 will become apparent as stage 3 draws to a close.

5.3   Building on existing contingency planning

Some organisations will already have undertaken contingency planning for certain business processes or functions, most often for IT systems and networks. If this is the case the organisation will already have accepted the need for BCM (albeit with a limited scope) and may have a management structure in place to support it.

Where existing contingency planning work has been undertaken it may be possible to build on this:

- a business impact analysis and risk assessment may already have been completed from which a business continuity strategy could be developed

- contingency plans may exist which could be extended to cover all parts of the business process

- testing, review, change control and education/awareness programmes may already be in place.

Care must, however, be taken to ensure that any existing contingency strategies and plans are consistent with the business-led approach of BCM. IT contingency plans that have been developed in isolation from the business processes they support may not meet the organisation's requirements or fit easily alongside recovery plans for other parts of the business process.

6 Generating awareness and commitment to business continuity management

Establishment of a successful BCM initiative will depend initially on the awareness and commitment of the Board and Senior Management and then on the acceptance and commitment of key managers and staff and the quality of contribution that they are able to make.

Ongoing success of the initiative will depend on a continuing commitment at all levels in the organisation and on people's awareness of their respective responsibilities.

6.1 Awareness of the need for BCM

Awareness of the need for BCM will come with a perception of:

- the range of risks facing an organisation and its vulnerability

- the potential business impacts that could result should any of the risks materialise

- the likelihood of each of the risks materialising

- personal responsibilities and liabilities

- external pressures, eg from regulators.

The St Mary Axe and Bishopsgate bombings in London crystallised for senior executives the risks from terrorism and many new business continuity initiatives followed in the wake of these attacks.

Although terrorism has often been the primary concern over recent years there are many other risks that could result in serious disruption to the business. In fact, incidents such as computer or telecommunications failures, failure of key suppliers, localised fires and floods have, collectively, caused much greater damage than high profile terrorist bombings.

The best way to raise awareness of the need for BCM is to highlight the potential risks and business impacts facing the organisation. Where possible, these should be stated in relation to key performance indicators, eg customer service levels, costs, turnover, profitability, market share.

If the potential impacts and risks are unclear or if there is some resistance to the concepts of BCM at senior levels then a useful first step may be to undertake a BCM Scoping Study. This will, typically, take no more than 10 to 15 days, and involve:

- listing important business processes and the risks of concern

- a high level business impact analysis

- listing any critical single points of failure

- where immediately apparent, listing some of the fall-back options for critical business processes or some of the options by which resilience may be improved.

The scoping report can then be used to raise awareness of the need for BCM, generate commitment and act as the starting point for more detailed project plans.

6.2   Commitment to the process

Once there is an awareness of the need for BCM and a project has been initiated, success will depend to a large extent on the co-operation and quality of input from key managers and staff. This will in turn depend upon:

- the existence of a high level sponsor

- the lead and direction given by the Board

- the priority attached to BCM in relation to other issues

- the calibre and credibility of the Project Manager and the Project Team.

The way in which the BCM message is communicated to those involved initially and the way in which the BCM project is conducted are therefore critical.

Initial briefing sessions are always worthwhile to raise awareness and engender support. Ideally, these will develop into an ongoing awareness campaign. Regular feedback to participants will also serve to demonstrate that progress is being made as a result of their contributions.

6.3   Continuing awareness

As an organisation moves through to stages 3 (Implementation) and 4 (Operational Management) of the BCM lifecycle emphasis extends from awareness of the need for BCM to include awareness of the responsibilities and actions necessary to invoke business recovery plans and to maintain the BCM deliverables.

Involvement of a wide range of staff in the development of business recovery plans will provide a good level of awareness and education and will also encourage ownership of BCM deliverables.

Organisations must protect their investment in BCM by ensuring that an ongoing programme of awareness, education and training is put in place. Used correctly, the testing programme is one way of educating and raising awareness for key individuals. For example:

- regular walkthroughs of business recovery plans will ensure that key staff remain aware of their responsibilities and the actions expected of them

- technical and functional tests will raise awareness and educate staff about potential problems and issues to be faced.

Awareness and education of deputies for key positions in the recovery teams will be very important and the testing programme must address this.

The following aspects of education and awareness may also be required:

- ongoing programme of briefings to all staff on the need for vigilance and on emergency procedures

- demonstration of stand-by facilities to selected staff, eg inspection of stand-by accommodation

- use of the organisation's newsletter to maintain the profile of BCM

- regular progress reports to the Board and a regular agenda item on other management committees.

Wherever possible senior management should be involved, to demonstrate commitment from the top. The overall aim must be to get to a stage where management considers business continuity issues in relation to and prior to making key business decisions. This will allow a balanced assessment of the risks to inform the decision making process.

In conclusion

BCM is essential in today's business environment, particularly where business processes are highly automated or heavily dependent on external service providers.

By taking a business led approach and focusing on defined risks BCM will protect the interests of staff, tax-payers, stakeholders, shareholders, customers, suppliers and the community at large.

Implemented properly, BCM is not expensive but a cost effective insurance policy against serious disruption to the business.

Can you afford to not have business continuity management?

Bibliography

CCTA volumes

CCTA is responsible for promoting the effective use of information systems in central government. It publishes a wide range of advice and guidance on issues of strategic importance that could affect the business and organisation of departments.

The following CCTA, and other relevant volumes, provide further information on topics covered in this guide.

IT Infrastructure Library Guides

The IT Infrastructure Library Guides are available from HMSO through its bookshops and agents as detailed on the back cover of this volume.

- Contingency Planning
  ISBN 0 11 330524 9

- Availability Management
  ISBN 0 11 330551 6

- Change Management
  ISBN 0 11 330525 7

- Configuration Management
  ISBN 0 11 330530 3

Management of Risk Library

The Management of Risk Library volumes are available from HMSO through its bookshops and agents as detailed on the back cover of this volume.

- Introduction to the Management of Risk
  ISBN 0 11 330648 2

- Management of Project Risk
  ISBN 0 11 330636 9

Programme and Project Management Library

The Programme and Project Management volumes are available from HMSO through its bookshops and agents as detailed on the back cover of this volume.

- An Introduction to Programme Management
  ISBN 0 11 330611 3

	• Guide to Programme Management ISBN 0 11 330600 8
PRINCE documentation	The PRINCE Reference Manuals (a set of five guides) are published by NCC Blackwell and are available from NCC Blackwell Ltd, Oxford House, Oxford Road, Manchester M1 7ED.
	• PRINCE Manuals ISBN 1 85554 012 6
	• PRINCE User's Guide to CRAMM ISBN 0 11 330596 6
Quality Management Library	The CCTA Quality Management Library is available as a set of five volumes from HMSO through its bookshops and agents as detailed on the back cover of this volume.
	• Quality Management Library ISBN 0 11 330569 9
Other CCTA documentation:	• BPR (Business Process Re-engineering) in the Public Sector ISBN 0 11 330651 2, HMSO (1994)
	• Guidelines for Directing Information Technology Security ISBN 0 946683 33 6 HMSO (1991)
Other publications	Survive! Magazine – Publisher, the Survive! Secretariat BS 7799: 1995 A Code of Practice for Information Security Management
Professional Development	The Business Continuity Institute (BCI), an industry-independent body, has been set up to provide an independently moderated and internationally recognised accreditation and certification scheme for business continuity professionals. Anyone wanting more information about the scheme should contact the institute at PO Box 4474, London SW18 3XB.

Glossary

Action lists	Defined actions, allocated to recovery teams and individuals, within a phase of a plan. These are supported by reference data.
Alert phase	The first phase of a business continuity plan in which initial emergency procedures and damage assessments are activated.
Asset	Component of a business process. Assets can include people, accommodation, computer systems, networks, paper records, fax machines, etc.
Assurance	The processes by which an organisation can verify the accuracy and completeness of its BCM.
BCM activity	An action or series of actions as part of a BCM process.
BCM process	A set of activities with defined deliverables forming a discrete part of the BCM lifecycle.
BCM lifecycle	The complete set of activities and processes necessary to manage business continuity – divided into four stages.
Business function	A business unit within an organisation, eg a department, division, branch.
Business process	A group of business activities undertaken by an organisation in pursuit of a common goal. Typical business processes include receiving orders, marketing services, selling products, delivering services, distributing products, invoicing for services, accounting for money received. A business process will usually depend upon several business functions for support, eg IT, personnel, accommodation. A business process will rarely operate in isolation, ie, other business processes will depend on it and it will depend on other processes.
Business recovery objective	The desired time within which business processes should be recovered, and the minimum staff, assets and services required within this time.

Business recovery plans	Documents describing the roles, responsibilities and actions necessary to resume business processes following a business disruption.
Business recovery plan framework	A template business recovery plan (or set of plans) produced to allow the structure and proposed contents to be agreed before the detailed business recovery plan is produced.
Business recovery team	A defined group of personnel with a defined role and subordinate range of actions to facilitate recovery of a business function or process.
CCTA	The Government Centre for Information Systems.
Command, control and communications	The processes by which an organisation retains overall co-ordination of its recovery effort during invocation of business recovery plans.
Contingency planning	Planning to address unwanted occurrences that may happen at a later time. Traditionally, the term has been used to refer to planning for the recovery of IT systems rather than entire business processes.
CRAMM	CCTA Risk Analysis and Management Method.
Crisis management	The processes by which an organisation manages the wider impact of a disaster, such as adverse media coverage.
Dependency	The reliance, either direct or indirect, of one process or activity upon another.
Disaster recovery planning	A series of processes that focus only upon the recovery processes, principally in response to physical disasters, that are contained within BCM.
Impact analysis	The identification of critical business processes, and the potential damage or loss that may be caused to the organisation resulting from a disruption to those processes. Business impact analysis identifies the form the loss or damage will take; how that degree of damage or loss is likely to escalate with time following an incident; the minimum staffing, facilities and services needed to enable business processes to continue to

operate at a minimum acceptable level; and the time within which they should be recovered. The time within which full recovery of the business processes is to be achieved is also identified.

Impact scenario

Description of the type of impact on the business that could follow a business disruption. Will usually be related to a business process and will always refer to a period of time, eg customer services will be unable to operate for two days.

Intelligent customer

The purchaser (as distinct from the provider) of services. The term is often used in relation to the outsourcing of IT/IS.

Invocation (of business recovery plans)

Putting business recovery plans into operation after a business disruption.

Invocation (of stand-by arrangements)

Putting stand-by arrangements into operation as part of business recovery activities.

Invocation and recovery phase

The second phase of a business recovery plan.

IS

Information Systems

IT

Information Technology

ITIL

The CCTA IT Infrastructure Library – a set of guides on the management and provision of operational IT services.

Maturity level/Milestone

The degree to which BCM activities and processes have become standard business practice within an organisation.

Outsourcing

The process by which functions performed by the organisation are contracted out for operation, on the organisation's behalf, by third parties.

Programme

A collection of activities and projects that collectively implement a new corporate requirement or function.

PRINCE	PRojects IN a Controlled Environment, the CCTA project management method.
Reference data	Information that supports the plans and action lists, such as names and addresses or inventories, which is indexed within the plan.
Return to normal phase	The phase within a business recovery plan which re-establishes normal operations.
Risk	A measure of the exposure to which an organisation may be subjected. This is a combination of the likelihood of a business disruption occurring and the possible loss that may result from such business disruption.
Risk reduction measure	Measures taken to reduce the likelihood or consequences of a business disruption occurring (as opposed to planning to recover after a disruption).
Self-insurance	A decision to bear the losses that could result from a disruption to the business as opposed to taking insurance cover on the risk.
Service level agreement	A formal statement of service characteristics between a demander and supplier of services.
Service provider	Third-party organisation supplying services or products to customers.
Stand-by arrangements	Arrangements to have available assets which have been identified as replacements should primary assets be unavailable following a business disruption. Typically, these include accommodation, IT systems and networks, telecommunications and sometimes people.

Printed in the United Kingdom for HMSO
Dd301866 1/96 C6 G3397 10170